BECOMING YOUR BEST SELF
100 QUOTES

COURAGE RESILIENCE AND GRATITUDE

CHRIS ANTHONY

Copyright 2024 Chris Anthony

All rights reserved. Published by Reach Out Recovery

No part of this publication may be reproduced, stored in a retrieval system, transmitted in any form by any means electronic, mechanical, photocopying, recording, or otherwise without prior written permission of the publisher and author/illustrator.

For information regarding permission contact us: thesoberexec.com (thesoberexec@gmail.com)

ISBN: 978-1-7324158-7-4

Printed in the U.S.A.
First printing January 2024
Book Design: Haley Laferney
Cover Design: Haley Laferney

DEDICATION

For Amy, Quinton, and Rowan. You are the prizes at the end of the rainbow. Family, friends, and coworkers that loved me, taught me, and have been patient with me.

CONTENTS

01	INTRODUCTION	7
02	BECOMING YOUR BEST SELF	9
03	COURAGE	10
04	RESILIENCE	39
05	GRATITUDE	81
06	ACKNOWLEDGEMENTS	119
07	ABOUT THE AUTHOR	121

INTRODUCTION

Over the span of my life's journey, I've gathered a unique collection—quotes. While some people collect tangible items, I've been drawn to the power of words. These simple arrangements of language manage to capture moments and feelings in a way that possessions can't quite replicate. This book holds 100 quotes about Courage, Resilience, and Gratitude, and it's not about following a strict plan. Think of it as a pocket guide for inspiration; you don't have to read it cover to cover. It's here to help whenever you need a boost or some guidance during life changes.

In my journey, I've learned that there are moments when I've recognized the need to make significant changes to create a better version of myself. These quotes are like little notes of encouragement for your path—reminders that in those pivotal moments, you have the power to shape your journey. But that's not all. Beyond the quotes, I've added optional affirmations and action prompts to nudge you a little closer to becoming your best self. So, let's dive in and explore the wisdom these words hold, accompanied by practical steps to enrich your journey, no matter where you are on life's adventure.

DISCLAIMER

Please be aware that the interpretations of the quotes in this book are uniquely my own, separate from any affiliation with organizations I am part of, and may not necessarily align with your own views. While I have diligently credited the original authors, there may be instances where quotes haven't been attributed accurately. It's crucial to understand that the inclusion of a quote in this book does not imply any endorsement of the quote author's beliefs or actions on my part.

THE ROAD TO BECOMING YOUR BEST SELF BEGINS WITH:

COURAGE

To embark on the journey toward your best self, we must first find the courage within ourselves to take that first step forward. It's only when we can conquer our fears and doubts that we can begin to unlock our true potential and achieve the success we've always dreamed of in life.

RESILIENCE

But the path to your best self is not an easy one. It's a long and winding road that's filled with countless obstacles and challenges that will test our resolve and resilience. We must stay strong and persevere through the tough times, for it's only by facing adversity head-on that we can grow and become stronger.

GRATITUDE

And yet, despite the difficulties we may face along the way, we must always remember to be grateful for the journey itself. It's not just about reaching the destination, but also about savoring every step of the way and appreciating the moments that make life worth living.

No matter what kind of personal excellence you are striving for, may these 100 Quotes, Affirmations, and Action Prompts ignite your courage, sustain your determination, and keep you grounded on your journey through this extraordinary thing we call life.

COURAGE

When you think about courage, what does it really mean to you? Courage can be defined as the inner strength to confront fear or endure pain and hardship. However, its meaning evolves throughout our lives. Sometimes, courage calls us to face significant and intimidating challenges, while other times, it's as simple as finding the resilience to carry on, even when we'd rather not.

Life, as we all know, is full of unexpected twists and turns. We can't foresee when we might lose a loved one or when life will throw us a curveball, demanding difficult decisions. Often, adversity strikes without warning, sometimes bringing life-or-death struggles. What we can count on, though, is that life's challenges are constant. That's the reason having inspiring words like these quotes, that have guided me through my own moments of need, can be so beneficial.

Courage is an integral part of the journey to becoming your best self because it often goes hand in hand with resilience. Resilience, the ability to bounce back from adversity and keep moving forward, is the sister of courage. When we face challenging situations with courage, we're not just enduring, but we're building resilience. We're learning to adapt and grow, to take those unexpected twists and turns in stride.

What's truly remarkable about courage is its versatility. Whether you've demonstrated bravery on a grand scale, saved lives, or simply brought comfort to someone in need, you're a living example of courage. Remember, courage doesn't demand that you conquer the world in a day. Right now, all you need is the courage to take that first step.

But here's a secret: courage is not just a one-time thing. It's like a skill you can nurture and strengthen over time. The more you practice being brave, the more resilient you become. So, when life presents its challenges, remember these principles of courage: be open to trying, keep learning, have faith in yourself, take action, and keep practicing. They'll be your compass as you navigate life one day at a time.

I hope these words serve as a source of inspiration for you as they have for me, guiding you through the intricate terrain of life. Courage and resilience, intertwined, will be your allies on the journey to becoming your best self.

"A journey of a thousand miles must begin with a single step."
— Lao Tzu

Affirmation

With each step, I build my confidence and diminish my fears. I am brave and determined to push through any obstacle that comes my way. The comfort of my past will not hold me back from achieving my dreams. I am ready to face the unknown with courage and determination. I am strong, courageous, and capable of achieving my goals.

Action Prompt

Reflect on what's weighing on your heart, whether it's a new beginning, a nagging problem, or a goal that's been eluding you. Identify the first step you can take today to address or tackle that issue. Write it down and commit to taking that crucial step forward. Remember, every great journey starts with that one small action.

_____
_____
_____
_____
_____
_____
_____
_____
_____
_____

> **"How many success stories do you have to hear before you write your own?"**
> –Unknown

Affirmation

I am capable of achieving success. The key to unlocking my own success is to take action and write my own story. It takes courage to pursue my dreams, to believe in myself, and to persist through obstacles. But with each step forward, I am closer to achieving my goals and creating my own success story. I will be inspired by the successes of others and use that inspiration to propel me forward towards my own.

Action Prompt

What do you want to be successful at? Whose story inspires you? If you could write your success story in a couple of lines how would it read?

_____
_____
_____
_____
_____
_____
_____
_____
_____
_____
_____

"Life expands or shrinks in proportion to one's courage."
- Anais Nin

Affirmation

I am the master of my own destiny, and I choose to embrace every opportunity that comes my way with courage and determination. I will be brave in the face of challenges and trust in my abilities to overcome them. Life is a journey, and I choose to make the most of it by being courageous and seizing every opportunity for growth and fulfillment.

Action Prompt

What challenge are you facing? Is there anyone or anything that could serve as an opportunity to help you face that challenge? How could you face a challenging situation with courage today?

_____
_____
_____
_____
_____
_____
_____
_____
_____
_____
_____

> **"You don't have to see the whole staircase, just take the first step."**
> – Martin Luther King, Jr.

Affirmation

With each step I take, the staircase reveals itself to me. Sometimes the destination may seem far away or uncertain, but the courage to take the first step is what propels me forward. The unknown can be scary, but with each step, the path becomes clearer, and the destination becomes more attainable. I have the courage to keep moving forward, one step at a time.

Action Prompt

Ask anyone who has found success and they will tell you things get done one step at a time. There is a process to attaining a goal or recovering from anything. They all happen one step at a time and one day at a time. What is one step to take today to further your efforts?

_____
_____
_____
_____
_____
_____
_____
_____
_____

"Too many of us are not living our dreams because we are living our fears."

– Les Brown

Affirmation

Today, I choose to break free from the chains of fear and embrace the path of courage. I will not allow my dreams to wither in the shadows of my doubts. Instead, I will take bold steps towards my aspirations. I will confront my fears and turn them into stepping stones toward my dreams. Each day, I will take actions that align with my aspirations, knowing that courage is the fuel propelling me forward.

Action Prompt

Identify a dream you've been afraid to pursue. Write it down. Recognize the specific fears holding you back. Choose one fear to confront and take a small action towards your dream right now.

_____
_____
_____
_____
_____
_____
_____
_____
_____

"Everything you ever wanted is on the other side of fear."
- Unknown

Affirmation

Everything I desire lies beyond the barriers of fear, and I am determined to break through those barriers and claim success. I have the strength and resilience to overcome any obstacle that comes my way. I will embrace each challenge as an opportunity to grow and become the best version of myself. Today, I am fearless, and nothing can hold me back.

Action Prompt

Take a moment to identify what you're afraid of right now. Then, write it down and visualize what lies beyond that fear. Explore the possibilities that await you once you step past that barrier.

_____
_____
_____
_____
_____
_____
_____
_____
_____
_____
_____
_____

> **"Sometimes in order to succeed the last thing you want to do is the first thing you need to do."**
> **- Unknown**

Affirmation

As I begin this day, I will not let the fear of failure hold me back from achieving my dreams. I will ask for help when I need it, and not let my pride stop me from reaching my full potential. I believe in myself and my abilities. With every step, I gain confidence and strength. I am courageous, and I am unstoppable.

Action Prompt

Identify a task or challenge that you've been avoiding because it seems daunting or uncomfortable. Take a proactive step today to start tackling that task, no matter how small. Remember, small wins stack up but you have to take that first step forward! Then repeat.

_____
_____
_____
_____
_____
_____
_____
_____
_____
_____
_____

"You miss every shot you don't take."
– Wayne Gretzky

Affirmation

Today, I will take my shot. I won't let fear hold me back from taking action. With each attempt, I get closer to success. I know that failure is not the opposite of success; it's a part of the journey towards it. The path to success may not be clear, but taking action is the first step toward making progress.

Action Prompt

What's the shot you're afraid to take today? Consider the following things: what would it look like and feel like to take it? How will you feel if it works out? How will you feel if it doesn't work out? What do you need today to help you find the courage to take that shot?

_____
_____
_____
_____
_____
_____
_____
_____
_____
_____
_____

"The cave you fear to enter holds the treasure you seek."
- Joseph Campbell

Affirmation

In the face of fear, I choose to step into the cave I dread. As I venture deeper into the unknown, I discover my strength, my resilience, my wisdom, and my hidden potential. With each courageous step, I commit to this journey of self-discovery, for it is within the depths of fear that I find the invaluable gems of my personal growth and courage.

Action Prompt

Reflect on your fears and identify a challenge you've been avoiding. Acknowledge the discomfort it brings. Now, summon the courage to take that first step into the feared territory. What courageous action can you take today to venture into the cave and discover those treasures?

_____
_____
_____
_____
_____
_____
_____
_____
_____
_____
_____

> "In any given moment we have two options: Step forward into growth or step back into safety."
> - **Abraham Maslow**

Affirmation

I choose to step forward into growth, leaving my comfort zone behind. Fear will not deter me from reaching my potential. I embrace the unknown, take risks with courage, and trust in my abilities. Challenges may arise, but through them, I grow stronger. I prioritize growth over safety and take that step forward on my journey toward greatness.

Action Prompt

Visualize the scenario where you take a leap of faith and venture outside your comfort zone, whether in your personal life, career, or any other aspect. How would it feel if you embraced the challenge and it led to success? Conversely, how would it feel if you never gave it a try? Reflect on these questions and take a small step forward today towards your growth.

_____
_____
_____
_____
_____
_____
_____
_____
_____
_____

> **"You are one decision away from a completely different life."**
> – Tony Robbins

Affirmation

Today, I have the courage to make the decision that will lead me toward the life I want. Fear won't hold me back from taking action and creating my best life. I trust myself to make the right choice, and I have faith that the universe will support me. I am ready to embrace the unknown and step out of my comfort zone.

Action Prompt

Recognize that within you both positive and negative aspects exist. It's what you choose to nurture that will thrive. Reflect on your goals and identify the decisions that will propel you closer to them, not further away. Comfort may seem appealing, but is it bringing you happiness? Today, pinpoint one decision you can make to cultivate the good within you and move closer to your goals.

_____
_____
_____
_____
_____
_____
_____
_____
_____

"What you put up with you end up with."
– Unknown

Affirmation
Today, I will not settle for less than I deserve and I will have the courage to speak up for myself. I choose to set my boundaries and stand firm in my values. By doing so, I create a life filled with respect, abundance, and joy. I will not let fear hold me back from demanding my worth.

Action Prompt
Sometimes we get comfortable in situations that aren't comfortable. There's a special feeling of sadness and defeat when you know you are living in any circumstance that is making you unwell. Is there anything you are putting up with that won't stop troubling you?

_____
_____
_____
_____
_____
_____
_____
_____
_____
_____
_____
_____
_____

"Don't complain about things you're not willing to change."
- Unknown

Affirmation

I have the power to make changes in my life. If there's something that is bothering me, I won't just complain about it. I'll take action to change it. I won't sit around and wait for someone else to fix it for me. I won't be held back by fear or doubt. I have the courage to face my challenges head-on and make the necessary changes to create the life I deserve.

Action Prompt

Is there anything you don't like about yourself? Do you complain about it? How often do you think about what you don't like or complain about it? Would you ever consider taking actions to change what you don't like?

_____
_____
_____
_____
_____
_____
_____
_____
_____
_____
_____
_____
_____

"Leap and the net will appear."
- Unknown

Affirmation
I trust that when I take the leap, the universe will catch me. I have the courage to face my fears and take risks, knowing that the reward is on the other side. I choose to live life boldly and without hesitation, knowing that every step I take towards my dreams brings me closer to the life I desire.

Action Prompt
Someone once told me you can't have fear and faith at the same time. Faith is such a huge part of courage because everything is uncertain. Will I succeed at this job? Will this relationship work out? Will I be safe in this situation? Rarely do we have any sense of how things will go. Is there a leap you're afraid to make?

_____
_____
_____
_____
_____
_____
_____
_____
_____
_____
_____
_____
_____

"It is what it is until you change it."
- Unknown

Affirmation

Today, I give myself permission to think about anything I want to change in my life. I won't pressure myself to make those changes today, but I will allow my mind the space to imagine life with the changes I want to make. I will give myself permission to imagine a world where those changes have been made. I will only permit my mind to run free with positivity.

Action Prompt

You have more power in your life than you think you do. Change is hard, but it's impossible without a roadmap. Is there anything you've been thinking about changing, doesn't matter how big? Could you write down in a few sentences what you want to change and what would need to happen to make it real? Don't do any of it yet. Just write it down.

_____
_____
_____
_____
_____
_____
_____
_____
_____
_____

"It is easy to be brave from a safe distance."
- AESOP

Affirmation
It's only by taking risks and pushing past our comfort zone that we can truly grow and achieve greatness. Today, I choose to be courageous and face any challenges that come my way. I won't let fear paralyze me. Instead, I'll embrace the unknown, trust in my abilities, and take that leap of faith.

Action Prompt
You never know how brave you can be until it's time to be brave. How do you handle tough situations? Fight or flight? Do you sit on the sideline and watch and let life happen? Or do you face the fight up close and personal? Which works out better for you?

_____

_____

_____

_____

_____

_____

_____

_____

_____

_____

_____

_____

> "How you think when you lose determines how long it will be until you win."
> - GK Chesterton

Affirmation

I choose to think positively and grow from my failures. Courage is not just about facing challenges but also about how I respond to setbacks. I will pick myself up and push forward with determination and resilience. With each failure, I learn and become stronger. I choose to maintain a positive and growth-oriented mindset, knowing that my thoughts have power.

Action Prompt

Failure is an important part of success, and happy, successful people will tell you they don't see failure as a setback. A failure is a valuable learning opportunity. How is your perspective and attitude when things don't work out the way you want them to? Is there anything you could tell yourself when things don't work out that would inspire you to keep pushing forward?

_____
_____
_____
_____
_____
_____
_____
_____

> "The magic you are looking for is in the work you are attempting to avoid."
> – Unknown

Affirmation

The magic I seek is not found in procrastination or inaction, but in the hard work and challenges that lie ahead. I choose to approach each task with a courageous attitude and embrace challenging opportunities. With each step I take towards my goals, I am closer to unlocking the magic that lies within me. I'm courageous, I'm capable, and I'm ready to do the work.

Action Prompt

Mountains are climbed one step at a time and goals, whether they are personal, professional or physical are also reached one day, one to-do item at a time. Along the way, it's critical to notice and celebrate the small wins. What are the tasks you need to get done right now? How about doing them and then celebrating that small win?

"Our character is what we do when no one is looking."
— J.C. Watts Jr.

Affirmation

I am not afraid to make difficult choices or stand up for what I believe in. I have the courage to uphold my values and principles, even in the face of adversity. With each decision I make, I am building a strong character that will serve me well throughout my life. I am committed to being a person of integrity, courage, and strength, even when no one is looking.

Action Prompt

Reflect on the moments when you've shown courage. How did you handle those situations? Now, challenge yourself to act with integrity, kindness, and bravery even when there's no audience. Embrace the opportunity to strengthen your character when the spotlight isn't on you. What courageous actions can you take today, regardless of who's observing?

_____
_____
_____
_____
_____
_____
_____
_____
_____
_____

"You either live life or life lives you."
– Unknown

Affirmation
Every day, I choose to embrace life with courage and intention. I seize opportunities, face challenges, and treasure each moment, for I understand that life is a precious gift. With courage as my guide, I will shape my destiny and create a life worth living. Today, I reaffirm my commitment to live life fully and authentically.

Action Prompt
Consider this: What is one small, courageous action you can take today to truly live life on your terms? Is there a decision you've been hesitating to make? Reflect and then commit to taking an action towards the goal. Embrace courage and take a step toward living life.

"Not all storms come to disrupt your life, some come to clear your path."
- Unknown

Affirmation

I embrace the storms that come my way. They clear my path and make space for new opportunities. I trust the process and have faith that the universe is working in my favor. I take a deep breath knowing that I'm not broken by storms that come my way, I'm made stronger by them.

Action Prompt

I've heard it said that you need a breakdown for a breakthrough. Sometimes bad things happen and it feels like your world is ending–that the rug is being snatched from beneath you. But, when the dust settles, sometimes those things weren't bad at all. They were path changers that needed to happen. Is there, or has there ever been, a storm like that in your life? Can you now see it differently? See any positives?

_____
_____
_____
_____
_____
_____
_____
_____

"Comfort zones are where dreams go to die."
- Unknown

Affirmation
Today, I embrace discomfort as a sign of growth and transformation. I commit to pushing the boundaries of my comfort zone, for it's the fertile soil in which my dreams will thrive. With each step, I am nurturing my aspirations and becoming the person I aspire to be.

Action Prompt
Identify a dormant dream or goal that your comfort zone has kept on hold. What small step can you take today to rekindle it? It might be a phone call, a plan, or seeking advice. Step out of your comfort zone and let your dreams flourish.

> **"Courage doesn't mean you don't get afraid. Courage means you don't let fear stop you."**
> – Unknown

Affirmation

Courage doesn't mean I won't feel afraid. Courage means I won't let fear hold me back. I am brave enough to face my fears and take action towards my goals. Even when I'm scared, I will choose to move forward with courage and determination. I will not allow fear to dictate my life. I am capable, courageous, strong, and unstoppable.

Action Prompt

Identify something you've been afraid to pursue or a challenge that intimidates you. Acknowledge that fear is a natural response. Now, muster your courage to take one step toward that goal. Embrace the idea that courage isn't the absence of fear, but the determination to keep going anyway. What courageous action can you take today, even if you're afraid?

_____
_____
_____
_____
_____
_____
_____
_____

"Don't be afraid your life will end. Be afraid it will never begin."
- Unknown

Affirmation
I will embrace each moment and take action towards my dreams. I will not be paralyzed by the thought of my life ending but instead be motivated to make the most of every opportunity. Life is precious, and I will live it fully with courage and determination. I choose to live a life without regrets, with each step forward taking me closer to the fulfillment of my potential.

Action Prompt
Reflect on something you've been postponing or a dream you've hesitated to chase. Embrace the fear that it might never come to fruition if you don't act. Now, harness your courage and take a meaningful step toward that goal. What courageous step can you take today to ensure your life begins?

_____
_____
_____
_____
_____
_____
_____
_____
_____
_____

"Insanity is doing the same thing, over and over again, but expecting different results."
– Albert Einstein

Affirmation

Today, I will have the courage to break free from my old patterns and try new approaches. I understand that growth requires stepping out of my comfort zone and taking risks. I will have the courage to try new things and learn from my mistakes. I will trust in my abilities and have the courage to keep moving forward, even when faced with challenges.

Action Prompt

Identify an area in your life where you've been stuck in a negative repeating cycle. Acknowledge the fear or hesitation holding you back. Now, summon the courage to break free from that pattern and try a new approach or a different perspective. What courageous action can you take today to shift your course and pursue different results?

_____
_____
_____
_____
_____
_____
_____
_____

"If you want something you've never had you'll have to do something you've never done."
- **Unknown**

Affirmation

Today, I am ready to step out of my comfort zone. I trust in my ability to learn, grow, and overcome challenges. I am determined, resilient, and courageous. I am creating a brighter, more fulfilling future for myself. I'm capable, worthy and unstoppable.

Action Prompt

Reflect on your aspirations, like your dream job or a fulfilling relationship. Identify the barriers holding you back, perhaps a lack of experience or skills. Now, consider one bold step you can take to overcome these hurdles. It could be enrolling in a professional class or reaching out to someone seemingly out of reach. Instead of fixating on external outcomes, focus on self-improvement for your own growth.

RESILIENCE

Exploring resilience reveals its intriguing duality. Resilience, defined as the ability to withstand and bounce back from difficulties, embodies both toughness and adaptability. To truly be resilient, you must possess the strength to stand firm when needed and the flexibility to adapt to ever-changing circumstances.

Resilience isn't just about weathering adversity; it's an essential component of your journey to becoming the best version of yourself. It's the cornerstone of personal growth, demanding courage and a gritty, resourceful spirit. Resilience encompasses both mental and physical aspects, vital for self-improvement.

As you embark on your journey toward self-improvement, you'll face obstacles and setbacks. Your resilience will guide you, helping you navigate these challenges, learn from them, and emerge stronger. Through my personal journey, I've discovered my resilience, facing the unknown with less fear, and honing my capacity to persevere.

Maintaining resilience requires inspiration and practice, supported by essential tools. Words, like quotes, ignite determination. Faith provides a solid foundation and a positive perspective. Rest, meditation, and mindfulness contribute to resilience.

Resilience becomes most challenging when our mental strength wavers, particularly during high-anxiety moments. Prioritizing emotional balance ensures resilience remains intact.

Your journey to becoming your best self relies on resilience, marked by growth and self-improvement. These tools and qualities will be your guiding light along this path.

"If you are going through hell, keep going!"
- Winston Churchill

Affirmation

On my journey, I know that I will encounter challenges that may feel insurmountable. I also know that I have the strength and resilience to persevere. Today, I know I am not alone, and that asking for help when I need it is a sign of strength, not weakness. I embrace the challenges, keep moving forward, and never hesitate to reach out for help if I need it.

Action Prompt

This quote is one of my favorites. Anyone who has been through tough times knows that you have to go through to get through. When you are feeling like you can't go on, what keeps you going? Do you need to do that now about something? Would it be possible to do it today?

_____
_____
_____
_____
_____
_____
_____
_____
_____

"Fall seven times, stand up eight."
- Unknown

Affirmation

Resilience is about getting up after every fall, no matter how many times it happens. I will stand up stronger, wiser, and more determined than before. It's okay to stumble and fall; it's a part of the journey. When life knocks me down, I won't stay down. I will stand up, brush off the dust, and keep moving forward with determination and resilience.

Action Prompt

What keeps knocking you down? Literally or metaphorically speaking. How do you take care of yourself when you get knocked down? What is one way you can take care of yourself today?

_____
_____
_____
_____
_____
_____
_____
_____
_____
_____
_____
_____
_____

"Life is full of obstacle illusions."
- Grant Frazier

Affirmation

Today, I will approach each challenge with a resilient mindset and see it as an opportunity for growth. I will focus on progress, not perfection, and celebrate each step forward towards my dreams. I am strong, determined, and worthy of success. I will start this day with a positive attitude, a grateful heart, and the courage to chase my dreams. I am unstoppable.

Action Prompt

Consider your desires, challenges, or new opportunities. Are there any perceived obstacles that might be rooted in fears, whether real or imagined? Identify them. Now, think of one practical way to ground yourself in reality and confront these fears today.

_____
_____
_____
_____
_____
_____
_____
_____
_____
_____

"I've never met a strong person with an easy past."
– Unknown

Affirmation
I am capable of overcoming any challenge or obstacle that comes my way. My past struggles have made me who I am and equipped me with the strength and resilience to face anything. I won't let fear or self-doubt hold me back from achieving my goals. I am unstoppable, resilient, and capable of achieving greatness. Today, I choose to be the best version of myself.

Action Prompt
Our pasts make us who we are. Surviving a tough past is exactly what can make a person resilient, strong, and inspirational. It's all about perspective and how you see what happened. Think about your past and consider what might be a good way to reframe it, if necessary. For example, what is one positive you can see as a result from tough times in your life?

_____
_____
_____
_____
_____
_____
_____
_____
_____
_____
_____
_____

> **"It does not matter how slow you go so long as you do not stop."**
> – Confucius

Affirmation

I won't let setbacks or obstacles hold me back from achieving my goals. Instead, I will take it one step at a time and celebrate each small victory along the way. I am committed to my end goal and won't give up until I succeed. I am strong, capable, and resilient, and I won't let anything stand in my way.

Action Prompt

The theme of one step at a time will come up throughout this book because that is how progress is made. One little action at a time. Getting through one day to do better the next. If you feel stuck with something you're working on or want to accomplish, what is one tiny step forward you could take today to get back on track?

_____
_____
_____
_____
_____
_____
_____
_____

"The struggle you're in today is developing the strength you need for tomorrow."

- **Unknown**

Affirmation

With resilience, I embrace the struggles of today, knowing that they are developing the strength I need for tomorrow. Each setback is an opportunity to grow stronger and wiser. I will not let fear or self-doubt hold me back from achieving my goals. Today, I am strong and resilient, and nothing can stand in my way.

Action Prompt

Everyone knows you don't eat the fruit the day you plant the tree. But, you plant that tree knowing fruit is coming your way down the line. As I mentioned earlier, being resilient is a practice and you get better at it as you see how you've survived in the past. What is one thing you can do today that would help you get your fruit down the line?

_____
_____
_____
_____
_____
_____
_____
_____
_____
_____
_____
_____

"Put your own oxygen mask on first."
- Unknown

Affirmation

I commit to prioritizing self-care for resilience. Just as airplane passengers secure their oxygen masks before helping others, I'll tend to my needs first. I'll take breaks, rest well, eat healthily, and embrace joyous activities. Today, I choose self-care to enhance my resilience and well-being.

Action Prompt

It's easy to get in the habit of taking care of others. But, think about how you feel when your own tank is out of gas? That's when we break down. This is about remembering to care for yourself. When you think about what you need, what comes to mind? Can you do it today? If not, what is one small action you can take towards getting what you need?

_____

_____

_____

_____

_____

_____

_____

_____

_____

"The bitter fruit of crisis bears the precious seed of growth."
- Unknown

Affirmation

Today, I won't be daunted by challenges, for they are opportunities for growth and learning. With patience and humility, I'll navigate through difficulties, confident that my resilience will guide me towards breakthroughs. My unwavering faith in the value of my efforts will see me through any adversity.

Action Prompt

Sometimes, the most valuable lessons arise from significant crises. While these moments can feel distressing, they are opportunities to exercise patience and faith. Is there a crisis in your life right now? How can you practice patience and maintain faith? What's one small action you can take today to bolster your patience?

_____
_____
_____
_____
_____
_____
_____
_____
_____
_____
_____

"Everyone has a choice in how they respond."
- Viktor Frankl

Affirmation

I am in control of my response to any situation, and I choose to respond with resilience. I will approach each challenge with a resilient mindset, knowing that my response can make all the difference. Today, I choose to respond with resilience, knowing that it will build the strength and character needed to overcome even the most difficult of situations.

Action Prompt

I don't know about you, but every single time I act unkind, entitled, or rude it comes back to haunt me. Karma is real. Not only does what goes around come around, but it feels better to take the high road. Don't take the bait today when life throws you an inconvenience. What is one way you can take the high road with someone or something that makes your blood boil?

_____
_____
_____
_____
_____
_____
_____
_____

"Every action you take is a vote for the type of person you wish to become."
- James Clear

Affirmation

Today, I am mindful that my actions shape my character and define my path. With unwavering determination, I cast my votes for kindness, empathy, and perseverance, paving the way for personal growth and positive change. I commit to being the best version of myself, one decision at a time, as I journey toward a life filled with purpose and fulfillment.

Action Prompt

Reflect on your recent actions and decisions. Are they in alignment with the kind of person you want to be? Identify one specific area where you'd like to make more intentional choices. What action can you take today to cast your vote for the person you aspire to become and cultivate resilience in the process?

_____
_____
_____
_____
_____
_____
_____
_____
_____

"Ninety-seven percent of the people who quit too soon are employed by the three percent that never gave up"

- Unknown

Affirmation

Today, I choose to be part of the three percent who never gave up and achieved their dreams. I won't let setbacks or failures discourage me from achieving my goals. Instead, I will approach each challenge with a never-give-up attitude, knowing that resilience is the key to success. With each setback, I will learn, adapt, and keep moving forward. I am capable of achieving greatness.

Action Prompt

It's often darkest before dawn, and that is when many people give up. You have to learn how to keep yourself motivated through the process, especially when you feel like quitting. How can you support yourself? What is one small act you could do to stay inspired today?

_____
_____
_____
_____
_____
_____
_____
_____
_____
_____

"When in doubt, breathe it out."
– Unknown

Affirmation

When feeling overwhelmed, I will take a moment to breathe and connect with my inner strength. I will let go of fear and doubt and approach challenges with a clear and level head. My breath will calm my mind, reduce stress, and increase focus, allowing me to persevere through the most challenging situations. Today, I choose to start the day with a deep breath and a resilient mindset.

Action Prompt

Box breathing is a valuable daily practice, and it also serves as a potent tool during moments of distraction. The method comprises four distinct steps, each lasting for four seconds: Inhale, hold your breath, exhale, then hold your breath again, and repeat. For optimal results, it is advisable to execute both the inhalation and exhalation phases through your nose.

"Take arrows in your forehead, but never in your back."
– Samurai Maxim

Affirmation

By taking responsibility for my actions, I will build trust, respect, and stronger relationships. Each challenge is an opportunity for growth and development, and I will use them to propel myself forward. Today, I start the day with a resilient mindset, embracing challenges with courage and determination.

Action Prompt

Think about a situation in your life where you may have been tempted to avoid confrontation or difficult conversations. How might you approach it differently now, aligning with the wisdom of this quote? What steps can you take to assertively address issues without compromising your principles or self-respect?

_____

_____

_____

_____

_____

_____

_____

_____

_____

_____

_____

_____

"Never mistake activity for achievement."
– John Wooden

Affirmation

It's essential to have a clear vision of what I want to achieve and take deliberate action with intention and purpose. By doing so, I can focus on the tasks that truly matter and make progress towards my goals. I won't mistake activity for achievement, for true achievement comes from deliberate and intentional effort. Each day, I will take purposeful action towards my goals, building resilience and achieving success in the process.

Action Prompt

Take a moment to examine your "to-do list" and make the critical distinction between tasks that truly contribute to your goals and those that can wait or be completed later. How can you prioritize the important tasks and streamline your efforts to ensure they align with your overarching goals?

_____
_____
_____
_____
_____
_____
_____
_____
_____
_____

"Relax. Everything is running right on schedule."
- The Universe

Affirmation

Today, I embrace the wisdom of the universe, understanding that everything unfolds as it should. I release anxiety and trust in the divine timing of life's events. I cultivate resilience by staying patient, confident, and adaptable in the face of challenges. I have faith that every step I take is part of my unique journey, leading to growth and success.

Action Prompt

Think of a challenging situation you're currently facing. How can you apply the wisdom of the quote 'Relax. Everything is running right on schedule' to your current circumstances? What small action can you take today to help you stay patient and confident while navigating this challenge?

_____
_____
_____
_____
_____
_____
_____
_____
_____
_____

"Worrying is literally betting against yourself."
- Unknown

Affirmation

Instead of worrying, I will focus on taking proactive steps towards my goals, knowing that I have the ability to succeed. By focusing on positive self-talk, I build the resilience needed to thrive in the face of adversity. Today, I choose to start the day with a positive mindset, trusting in my abilities, and focusing on proactive steps towards my goals.

Action Prompt

I have a friend who says, "Worrying is manifesting what you don't want to happen." While some of us are wired to worry, it doesn't inspire our minds. The trick is to notice when you're worried and replace those thoughts with positive ones. Instead of what if it doesn't work out? Think, "What if it does work out!" What is one constant worry you have and a thought you can replace it with?

_____
_____
_____
_____
_____
_____
_____
_____

"It's not the mountain we conquer, but ourselves."
– Sir Edmund Hillary

Affirmation

In every endeavor, I recognize that the true conquest lies within me, not just in external obstacles. The mountains I face are mirrors reflecting my inner strength, resilience, and growth. With each climb, I conquer self-doubt and limitations, unveiling my untapped potential. Today, I embark on the journey of self-conquest with determination and unwavering courage.

Action Prompt

Recognize that the true conquest lies within, not in external challenges. What internal barriers, such as self-doubt or fear, might impede your progress? Take a moment to consider, or journal, how you can overcome these inner obstacles and take concrete steps today to move closer to your goal.

_____
_____
_____
_____
_____
_____
_____
_____
_____
_____

"Any person capable of angering you becomes your master."
- Epictetus

Affirmation
I understand that my emotional state is crucial to my success, and I will maintain a clear and level head, even in the face of provocation. By maintaining emotional control, I stay focused on my goals. I am the master of my emotions, and I won't let anyone else control them. Today, I choose to start the day with a commitment to emotional control and resilience.

Action Prompt
This is one of my favorite quotes because it is the best reminder that letting other people have power over your emotions is a disaster waiting to happen. It takes so much practice to not take things personally or have your feelings hurt, but it is so worth it if you can master being in control of your emotions. Who or what sets you off course? What is one small thing you can do today to maintain control of your own feelings?

_____
_____
_____
_____
_____
_____
_____
_____

> "**Confidence is not walking into a room and thinking you are better than everyone. Confidence is walking in and not having to compare yourself to anyone at all."**
> – Neil Strauss

Affirmation

Resilience requires self-confidence that is rooted in self-assurance. I won't base my self-worth on external validation or comparison, instead I value my uniqueness. I believe in myself and my abilities and will approach each challenge with confidence and determination, knowing that comparison will only rob me of my joy.

Action Prompt

Compare and despair! It is useless comparing yourself to anyone because we're all different. Have you noticed you compare? What is one thing you can say to yourself when you find yourself doing that to stop the comparison and focus on your own progress?

_____
_____
_____
_____
_____
_____
_____

"Success is the progression of a worthy ideal."
- Earl Nightingale

Affirmation
I will set realistic and attainable goals that align with my values and aspirations. I will take consistent and deliberate action towards achieving these goals, knowing that the journey towards greatness requires patience, persistence, and resilience. Today, I commit to resilience, embracing the process of continuous improvement.

Action Prompt
Every step forward, no matter how small, is a mark of success on the path toward your worthy ideal. So, acknowledge and celebrate any forward movement, recognizing that it's a valuable part of your journey, making every accomplishment, no matter the size, a success in its own right.

_____
_____
_____
_____
_____
_____
_____
_____
_____
_____
_____

"The pain will leave once it's finished teaching you."
- **Unknown**

Affirmation

I will embrace pain as a teacher on my journey to greatness. Pain can be a powerful catalyst for growth, helping me develop resilience, strength, and perseverance. Today, I choose to start the day with a commitment to embracing pain as a learning opportunity, knowing it will help me on my journey toward my goals.

Action Prompt

I've also heard it said that pain is the spiritual touchstone to growth. Do you feel emotional pain about anything in your life, or are there life lessons leaving you blue? How are you handling that pain? In healthy or unhealthy ways? What is one thing you can do today to support yourself in a healthy way through the pain.

_____
_____
_____
_____
_____
_____
_____
_____
_____
_____

"The only easy day was yesterday."
– **Unknown**

Affirmation
Every day presents new opportunities for growth and learning, and I'm committed to facing these challenges with enthusiasm. I won't be discouraged by setbacks but will approach them with a positive mindset, knowing that with resilience, persistence, and hard work, I can overcome any obstacle and achieve my goals.

Action Prompt
Isn't it the best when you push yourself when you don't feel like it and you make it through? That's what you need to remember when you start thinking something will be easier to do tomorrow. It isn't easier tomorrow, it's harder. Do it today and feel great after. What don't you want to do today? What's one small thing you can do to get you towards doing it?

> **"When I look back on all these worries, I remember the story of the old man who said on his deathbed that he had had a lot of trouble in his life, most of which had never happened."**
> - Winston S. Churchill

Affirmation

I embrace the present and let go of unnecessary concerns, I cultivate strength and clarity to overcome any challenges that may arise. Today, I choose to live in the moment, free from the weight of needless worries, and build my resilience to face the future with confidence and determination.

Action Prompt

Do you find yourself worrying excessively about things that seldom happen? Resilience thrives on positivity, not catastrophizing. How can you shift your mindset to focus on the positive? What small step can you take today to embrace optimism?

_____
_____
_____
_____
_____
_____
_____
_____

> **"When you talk about something, it's a dream. When you envision it, it's exciting. When you plan it, it's possible. But, when you schedule it, it's real."**
> - Tony Robbins

Affirmation

I will not just talk about my goals, but I will envision them and plan for their achievement. By scheduling my plans, I will bring them to life and make them a reality. Challenges may arise, but with resilience as my guide, I will persevere and overcome. Today, I choose to take action towards my dreams, and I believe in my ability to achieve them.

Action Prompt

Setting goals and having dreams is wonderful, but what's your roadmap to success? How do you plan to achieve them? Let these questions ignite your inspiration. If you committed to taking one step each day, what would your first step be?

_____
_____
_____
_____
_____
_____
_____
_____

> **"One day you will tell your story of how you overcame what you are going through and it will be someone else's survival guide."**
> - Brene Brown

Affirmation

My struggles will not define me, but my ability to overcome them will. I will not give up in the face of adversity, but instead, I will persist and emerge stronger on the other side. I choose to embrace my resilience and use it as a tool to help others who may be struggling. Today, I am a survivor, and I will use my strength to inspire those around me.

Action Prompt

It's universally true that we all desire love and understanding. When you share your experiences with someone facing similar challenges, you offer a beacon of hope and a sense of being understood. Is there someone who has been through what you're experiencing whom you could seek guidance from? Alternatively, if you're in a position to help someone else, how might you extend that support?

_____

_____

_____

_____

_____

_____

"No one can make you feel inferior without your consent."
– Eleanor Roosevelt

Affirmation
I choose to believe in myself and my abilities, even in the face of criticism or negativity. I will not let the opinions of others bring me down or hold me back. Instead, I will focus on my own self-confidence and inner strength. Today, I choose to cultivate resilience and self-belief, knowing that I have the power to control my own happiness and success.

Action Prompt
While insensitivity can be painful, the depth of its impact depends on your response. Recognize that you can't control others, and their words or actions may affect your self-esteem. How do you typically react when others make you feel inferior? What can you do or say to reassure yourself that you're okay and that their behavior reflects more on them than on you?

_____

_____

_____

_____

_____

_____

_____

_____

_____

_____

> **"Your value doesn't decrease based on someone's inability to see your worth."**
> – **Unknown**

Affirmation

I believe in myself and my abilities, even in the face of rejection or disapproval. I will not let external factors affect my sense of self-worth or determination. Instead, I will focus on cultivating self-love and confidence, knowing that I am worthy of success and happiness. Today, I choose to embrace my inner strength and I will not let anyone else define my worth.

Action Prompt

Consider situations where you've felt undervalued or underestimated by others. Reflect on how you typically respond to these moments. What action can you take today to remind yourself of your worth, independent of other's opinions? How can you reinforce your self-esteem and self-worth in such situations?

_____
_____
_____
_____
_____
_____
_____
_____
_____
_____

"No escape routes!"
– Unknown

Affirmation

I will not run away from my problems or seek an easy way out. Instead, I will confront my challenges with determination and inner strength. I am capable of handling hard things. By facing my challenges, I am building my toughness and becoming a stronger version of myself. Today, I embrace my challenges, knowing that they are opportunities for growth and learning.

Action Prompt

Let's be honest with ourselves: We all have our escape routes, ways we avoid challenges or cut corners. It's important to recognize them and gain clarity. Take a moment to identify your escape routes in life, whether in your work or personal life. Then, think about one small change you can make to help you stay on course and resist the temptation to seek that trap door. What's your strategy for staying committed and focused on your goals?

_____

_____

_____

_____

_____

_____

_____

_____

"You don't rise to the occasion you fall to the level of your preparation."
- U.S Navy SEAL Mantra

Affirmation

Today, I prepare for challenges, rising above with resilience. Not reliant on circumstances, but on my readiness. I build my strength, mentally and emotionally. I respond to life's tests with resilience, capable of overcoming all. Each challenge adds to my experience, strengthening my resilience.

Action Prompt

What steps can you take today to ensure that your preparation and resilience align with your aspirations? Think about your goals and the preparation required to reach them. Identify one area where you could improve your preparation, and outline a plan to enhance your readiness. Remember, you don't rise to the occasion; you fall to the level of your preparation. How can you properly prepare for success?

_____
_____
_____
_____
_____
_____
_____
_____
_____

"If you want to take the island, burn the boats."
– Tony Robbins

Affirmation

Just like burning the boats implies a complete commitment to a goal, I too am willing to make sacrifices and go all in to achieve my dreams. By fully committing myself, I am not only demonstrating my determination but also building my resilience. With each obstacle I overcome, I become a stronger, more resilient version of myself. Today, I embrace the journey towards my dreams, and I am fully committed to making them a reality.

Action Prompt

It's easy to talk a big game, but what are you willing to do to reach your goals? Are you making any sacrifices right now to help yourself reach your goal? If not, why not? If so, how do you stay inspired every day to keep making the sacrifice? Is there one small thing you could add to the mix to keep yourself resilient?

"You can learn a lot from your mistakes when you aren't busy denying them."

- **Unknown**

Affirmation

Today, I embrace getting real with myself and owning my mistakes. I commit to learning and growing. I will feel proud and confident that my work is valuable however it plays out. If I feel badly or ashamed I will turn it around quickly because failing is part of the process.

Action Prompt

Many have told me that our mistakes and failures are our greatest teachers. How do you handle it when you make a mistake or have a failure? Is there any mistake or failure that you can't stop thinking about? Can you see a lesson from what happened?

_____
_____
_____
_____
_____
_____
_____
_____
_____
_____
_____

"Whatever you are not changing you are choosing."
- Unknown

Affirmation
I choose to actively make changes and cultivate perseverance. I am not content with accepting the status quo. Instead, I take control of my life and work towards my goals. Each change strengthens my perseverance, equipping me to handle whatever challenges I face. I commit to making the necessary changes to achieve my dreams.

Action Prompt
What or who is causing you distress? What have you been enduring or tolerating? This is your signal that change is within reach. While change might not happen overnight, it's always possible. Identify something you'd like to alter. What's required to make that change? What's one step you can take today to support yourself in this process?

_____

_____

_____

_____

_____

_____

_____

_____

_____

_____

"You have to stop watering dead plants."
- **Unknown**

Affirmation

I affirm my commitment to resilience by recognizing the importance of letting go of unproductive or unhealthy situations. I choose to redirect my efforts towards nurturing what truly matters, focusing on positive, life-affirming opportunities. By releasing what no longer serves me, I create space for resilience and personal growth. Today, I prioritize my resources and energy, nurturing the aspects of my life that empower my journey.

Action Prompt

Do you have anything in your life that you know isn't good for you? It could be relationships, work, habits, addictions, or any other negative source. On your journey to greatness, you should focus your energy on things that have the potential to grow and thrive. Reflect on anything in your life that doesn't serve you. What would it look like to get rid of it or make a change?

_____
_____
_____
_____
_____
_____
_____
_____

"The fact that you are still here is proof that whatever tried to beat you lost."

- Unknown

Affirmation

Today, I celebrate my toughness and inner strength. I am capable of overcoming any obstacle that comes my way. My past struggles do not define me; rather, they made me stronger and more tenacious. I take pride in my ability to persevere and rise above adversity. I won't let the challenges of today hold me back. Instead, I will embrace them as opportunities to grow and become even more resilient.

Action Prompt

Look at everything you've overcome in your life. What would it look like to celebrate that today? Instead of the usual worry or time for self-improvement, what's one thing you can do today to take care of yourself and make yourself feel special?

_____
_____
_____
_____
_____
_____
_____
_____
_____

> "You have within you right now, everything you need to deal with whatever the world can throw at you."
> – Brian Tracy

Affirmation

Today, I know that I am competent and capable. I have the skills to handle whatever comes my way in life. If something big comes up, I remember I can pause and think through a solution, even ask for help. I will not be overwhelmed, for I know I am capable of taking care of myself.

Action Prompt

You possess far more strength than you realize. Reflect on your life and recall times when you've supported friends, excelled at work, or been there for others. Don't always trust your own doubts. What's currently causing you stress in your life? Now, catalog all your exceptional qualities. Identify which of these qualities will be crucial in addressing the stressful situation.

_____

_____

_____

_____

_____

_____

_____

_____

_____

> **"Reminder: you have survived one hundred percent of all the bad days in your life. You will get through this."**
> – Unknown

Affirmation

I choose to focus on the present and take each day as it comes, knowing that I have the power to overcome anything. I will not let fear or doubt hold me back. I will embrace my inner strength and resilience. Today, I choose to be grateful for my past successes and use them to find the strength to get through current challenges. I believe in myself and my abilities.

Action Prompt

So many little things can throw you off throughout the day and ruin your mood or make you feel like low, but you have reference from all the bad days you got through. Use that reference to remind yourself that you are strong. You are a survivor! What is one thing you can do today to honor the survivor in you?

_____
_____
_____
_____
_____
_____
_____
_____
_____

"Life is unfair. Accept that fact."
- Unknown

Affirmation

Today, I will focus on cultivating inner strength and determination to face challenges that comes my way. I choose to embrace the ups and downs of life, knowing that they are opportunities for growth. I will not let the unfairness of life define me or my path. I acknowledge reality and find the motivation to keep moving forward.

Action Prompt

This is a hard pill to swallow because it's normal to want life to be fair, especially if you are someone who cares about right and wrong. So, it's extra important to find ways to be OK when life gets unfair. Is there anything you can think of that keeps you strong when you feel life is unfair? Is there something you can do today to help yourself be in acceptance?

_____
_____
_____
_____
_____
_____
_____
_____
_____
_____

"The temptation to quit will be the greatest just before you are about to succeed."
- Chinese Proverb

Affirmation

I will stay committed to my goals and dreams, even when it feels difficult or overwhelming. Success may be just around the corner, and I will not let the temptation to quit hold me back. I will use any setbacks or obstacles as opportunities to grow and learn. I choose to embrace the journey towards my goals, knowing that it will take hard work and determination.

Action Prompt

It's always darkest before the dawn. That's why you have to prepare and be at your strongest for when that temptation sneaks in. What do you do when life is most difficult? What is one way you can take care of yourself today to keep yourself from quitting?

_____
_____
_____
_____
_____
_____
_____
_____
_____
_____
_____

"The day you plant the seed is not the day you eat the fruit."
– Fabienne Fredrickson

Affirmation

Today, I will not expect immediate results, but instead, I will nurture my dreams with hard work and determination. I choose to stay committed to my goals, even when it feels difficult or overwhelming. I know that success doesn't come overnight. I will focus on the journey towards my goals, knowing that with time and effort, I will see the fruit of my labor.

Action Prompt

This is an important reminder that the work you're doing today is for a better tomorrow. You may not feel wonderful, or see progress, when you first you start working towards a goal. So, it's crucial to keep perspective. What is something you can do to keep your perspective while you're climbing the mountain and don't see the top?

_____
_____
_____
_____
_____
_____
_____
_____
_____

GRATITUDE

What is your relationship with gratitude? If you're familiar with the benefits of gratitude, these quotes won't be news to you. But if you're new to the concept, this chapter can be a transformative journey towards becoming your best self.

Gratitude isn't just a feel-good emotion; it's a fundamental step on the path to self-improvement. It might not come naturally to most of us, as we often focus on our desires and what we lack. However, learning to live in gratitude can be a game-changer.

Practicing gratitude has a profound impact on your daily life and mood. When you practice gratitude, your brain releases serotonin and dopamine, those wonderful feel-good chemicals. You'll find yourself less stressed and happier. You'll radiate positive energy, attracting better opportunities and people into your life.

But remember, gratitude is a skill that requires practice. One of the best ways to nurture gratitude is by serving others. Helping and showing kindness not only benefits them but also builds your self-esteem and appreciation for what you have. Gratitude is an essential element of personal growth, helping you on your journey to becoming the best version of yourself.

Incorporating gratitude into your life costs nothing but can offer everything. It's a simple yet powerful tool that can change your perspective and enhance your well-being. So, dive into this chapter with an open heart, and let gratitude become your companion on the path to self-improvement.

"The joy is in the journey, not at the end of it."
– Unknown

Affirmation

Today, I will remember that I gain joy in every step of my journey. I will embrace the process and enjoy experiencing the present moment. I will take pleasure in the day-to-day. I will empower myself to love the ride and acknowledge every little piece of progress along the way. I will feel happy knowing that I'm doing only what I need to do today.

Action Prompt

The greatest artists and creators will confirm that you must love the journey of creating. You can't hold your breath as you work towards what you want. Enjoying the process, the practice and the creating will help you feel good every day, not just when the job is done. What is one small thing you do, or can do every day to make the journey more enjoyable?

_____
_____
_____
_____
_____
_____
_____
_____
_____
_____

"Gratitude turns what you have into enough."
- AESOP

Affirmation

Today, I remind myself to approach my goals with a mindful attitude, appreciating every step. I know that I will find joy and fulfillment in the present moment, knowing that I am exactly where I need to be. With each breath, I embrace a sense of contentment and gratitude, knowing that this attitude will carry me through any challenges.

Action Prompt

If you don't have gratitude for what you have now, you won't have gratitude for what you want. Gaining courage, resilience or gratitude is not about waiting for the perfect opportunity or experience, it's about starting right now. The practice of being grateful can start small, but it must start now. What are you grateful for that you have today? List five things.

"Hating yourself will never get you as far as loving yourself."
- Unknown

Affirmation

Today, I embrace my imperfections so I am able to show up more fully in the world and in my relationships. I choose to cultivate a deep sense of self-acceptance and appreciation for all that I am. With each breath, I allow love to fill my heart and guide me on this journey. I am worthy, I am loved, and I am enough.

Action Prompt

Self-love and self-acceptance are mandatory for a happy, healthy life. It might be hard at first, especially if you're not used to it. But, learning to love yourself will help you get where you want to go. It's not all about hard work and the outside things, the inside needs nurturing and love too. How can you show yourself love? What is one self-love gift you can give yourself?

> "When you change the way you look at things, the things you look at change."
>
> - Wayne Dyer

Affirmation

Today, I shift my perspective and focus on the positive, so that I am empowered to see possibilities and potential where others see limitations. With each breath, I embrace a new perspective and allow myself to be open to the infinite opportunities that life has to offer.

Action Prompt

A healthy perspective will transform your life. When you are lost in your fears, take a step back. Look at the big picture and give yourself some perspective to clear away the worry. Is there one situation troubling you? Will looking at if from another angle help? What is one way you can change your POV on what's troubling you?

> **"If you see no reason for giving thanks, the fault lies in yourself."**
> – Native American Proverb

Affirmation

Today, I embrace a thankful attitude, so that I am able to see the good in even the most challenging situations and approach my journey to greatness with a sense of appreciation and joy. With each breath, I cultivate a sense of gratitude and abundance, knowing that this attitude will bring more blessings into my life.

Action Prompt

When times are tough I like to remind myself of all the people all over the world who would kill for what I have – the freedoms, the roof over my head, available food and water. Many don't have any of that. What do you have to give thanks for today? Make a short list of how abundant your life is compared to those who are suffering.

_____
_____
_____
_____
_____
_____
_____
_____
_____
_____

"Gratitude helps you see what's there instead of what isn't."
— Unknown

Affirmation

Today, I focus on what's there instead of what isn't, recognizing the gifts that I've been given. By approaching life with a sense of appreciation and thankfulness, I am able to find contentment and joy in the present moment. With each breath, I embrace a new perspective, and allow myself to see the beauty and potential in every situation. I am grateful for all that I have.

Action Prompt

In 2019, I started a daily gratitude practice, jotting down three things I was thankful for each day. I continued this habit until one stressful day when I mindlessly listed my biggest stressors. Surprisingly, it shifted my perspective, and I realized they weren't as terrible as I thought. I learned that even in challenges, I could find hidden gifts. Have you acknowledged the gifts in your life? Can you make a simple list of them today?

_____

_____

_____

_____

_____

_____

_____

_____

_____

"Someone else is praying for the things you take for granted."
- Unknown

Affirmation

Today, I will reframe my perspective and focus on the positive aspects of my life. I will help others by volunteering, donating, or spreading kindness. I will remember to empathize with others and understand their struggles and challenges. I know I can cultivate an attitude of humility by recognizing that blessings come from a higher power and not just personal achievement.

Action Prompt

There is a lot about society that encourages us to want more. Yet, a key to happiness is staying grateful for what we have. What do you have today that you once longed for? Are you overlooking anyone or anything in your life? How can you show appreciation for what you have today?

_____
_____
_____
_____
_____
_____
_____
_____
_____
_____

"Anything you "get" will never be greater than the things you do."
- Unknown

Affirmation
Today, I focus on my actions and the positive impact I can have on the world. By cultivating a sense of gratitude and mindfulness, I recognize the importance of my choices and the power I hold to create positive change. With each breath, I embrace a sense of purpose and commitment to making a difference, knowing that this is the true path to greatness.

Action Prompt
Think about the things you've been given versus the things you earned or got for yourself. Which were more meaningful? If you're like me, it's always the things you worked hard for, put the time in, and earned for yourself. What are you working on for yourself? What is one small way to stay inspired and humble while you're working towards your goal?

_____
_____
_____
_____
_____
_____
_____
_____
_____
_____
_____

"Would you like you if you met you?"
- Unknown

Affirmation

Today, I challenge myself to become the kind of person that I would like to meet. By cultivating a sense of gratitude and mindfulness, I prioritize kindness, empathy, and compassion in all that I do. I strive to create positive change in the world, both in my achievements and in the kind of person I become. I commit to being a person that I admire and respect.

Action Prompt

Do you think about how you seem to other people? You don't want to be obsessed with what other people think, or let their opinions drive you. On the other hand, it's good to know how you seem out there in the world. Are you likable? Do you make others feel comfortable? What's one way you could be kind to someone else today?

_____
_____
_____
_____
_____
_____
_____
_____
_____
_____
_____

"Remember that everyone you meet is afraid of something, loves something, and has lost something."
- Proverb

Affirmation

Today, I approach every interaction with empathy and understanding, recognizing the humanity in everyone. I commit to creating positive change in the lives of those around me, and strive to be a source of kindness and compassion in the world. I embrace the power of empathy and understanding, and commit to making a difference in the world.

Action Prompt

Next time someone annoys you, remember that they might be in a terrible situation. It's important to give others the same leeway we want when we're having a tough time. How can you be open to the stories of others, and honor the rich tapestry of human experience that surrounds you? Who can you listen to today?

> **"Be kind, for everyone you meet is fighting a hard battle."**
> – Unknown

Affirmation

Today, I commit to being a source of support and compassion in the world. With each breath, I cultivate gratitude and mindfulness. I affirm that I will make a positive impact and strive to create a compassionate and connected world. I am grateful for the opportunity to be kind and empathetic, knowing these small acts can have a big impact.

Action Prompt

It's challenging to remember this in the heat of the moment, like when someone cuts you off on the road. However, it's important to consider that they might be rushing to an emergency. We all face challenges, and some are more difficult than others. Is there a reminder that can help you practice kindness throughout your day?

_____
_____
_____
_____
_____
_____
_____
_____
_____
_____

> "Do not spoil what you have by desiring what you have not; remember that what you now have was once among the things you only hoped for."
> – **EPICURUS**

Affirmation

Today, I focus on the present and cultivating a sense of gratitude so I am able to fully appreciate the gifts in my life. With each breath, I embrace a sense of contentment and joy. I celebrate the hard work and dedication that has brought me to where I am, and approach the future with a sense of hope and excitement.

Action Prompt

Isn't it amazing how badly you can want something, then you get it and soon you want something else? Such is human nature. But, the problem with the more more more mentality is that it takes you out of the present. What do you have today that you used to want? How can you appreciate those things today?

"Talk to yourself like you would to someone you love."
– Brene Brown

Affirmation

Today, I choose self-compassion and self-love on my path to greatness. I affirm my worthiness of love and acceptance. I commit to self-kindness and respect. I choose to speak to myself as I would to someone I love, unlocking my potential and finding personal fulfillment.

Action Prompt

A friend once asked, "Would you talk to a friend the way you talk to yourself?" I was shocked and said, "Never!" She replied, "Then why do you talk to yourself that way?" It's worth considering. What's your inner dialogue like? Is there a way you could be kinder to yourself today?

_____
_____
_____
_____
_____
_____
_____
_____
_____
_____
_____
_____

"Love and knowledge are two things you can give away yet still keep."
- Chuck Hillig

Affirmation
Today, I commit to sharing my love and knowledge with those around me, creating a ripple effect of positivity and growth in the world. By giving away these gifts freely, I do not lose anything myself, but instead, gain a deeper sense of personal fulfillment and purpose. I am a source of love and knowledge in the world, and this is the true path to greatness.

Action Prompt
Emotionally healthy people know that to give love is as important as it is to receive love. The same goes for knowledge. You actually receive more knowledge and love when you give it away. How are you sharing love and knowledge? What is one small thing you can do today to share love or knowledge with the people around you?

"It costs $0.00 to be a nice person."
- Unknown

Affirmation

I commit to creating a more kind and connected world, one small act of kindness at a time. I remember that being a nice person is not only free, but also the true path to greatness. I choose to be a source of kindness and compassion in the world, knowing that this is the most valuable gift I can give. I remember to say nothing if I have nothing nice to say, and I commit to spreading positivity in all of my interactions.

Action Prompt

The happiest man on earth, a French Buddhist monk named Ricard, believes the secret to happiness is compassion. And not just for the people you care about, but for everyone. If the key to happiness costs nothing, why not use it? Be kind, be compassionate, care for those around you. How can you practice this today?

> **"When you see something beautiful in someone tell them. It might take a second to say but for them it could last a lifetime."**
> **- Unknown**

Affirmation

I cherish the happiness that comes from spreading kindness and celebrating the beauty in those around me. I choose to be a source of love and positivity, knowing that gratitude can transform lives. With the power of small acts of kindness, I am dedicated to making the world better, one grateful and kind word at a time.

Action Prompt

In your gratitude journey, remember the value of your kind words to others. Everyone seeks to be seen and appreciated. How can you express appreciation for the beauty you see in someone today?

_____
_____
_____
_____
_____
_____
_____
_____
_____
_____

"Be kind whenever possible. It is always possible."
– Dalai Lama

Affirmation

Today, I embrace the power of empathy and compassion, knowing that these small acts have the ability to create positive change in the world. I remember that kindness is an infinite well that I can draw from endlessly. By choosing kindness, I choose the path to greatness, and I spread positivity and kindness wherever I go.

Action Prompt

Being grateful and positive becomes a lifestyle when you make it a routine in your life. At first, you have to remember to be kind, then you practice it, then it becomes second hand. Are there ways you could be kinder to people in your life? What's one thing you can do today to make a start?

_____
_____
_____
_____
_____
_____
_____
_____
_____
_____

"Comparison is the thief of joy."
- Unknown

Affirmation
Today, I will focus on my own growth and journey. I will stop evaluating my own life, abilities, and possessions in relation to others and feel confident and proud of what I have. I know what I have is enough and everything I want and am working for is coming. I love everything I am and have and don't need to compare myself to anyone or anything.

Action Prompt
Avoid the "compare and despair" trap. Comparing yourself to others often leads to unhappiness, as everyone's life is unique. Today, consider taking a break from social media to enhance your focus on personal progress. What actions can you take to prioritize your own journey and well-being today?

"True humility is not thinking less of yourself; it is thinking of yourself less."
— C.S. Lewis

Affirmation

Today, I will practice humility by seeking to understand and empathize with others' perspectives. I will practice self-reflection and self-awareness to recognize and challenge negative thoughts and behaviors. I am open to feedback and criticism, recognizing that it can help me grow. I will also volunteer or help others in need, putting their needs before my own.

Action Prompt

I used to think that because I was low on self-esteem that I couldn't be self-centered. Well, if you think about yourself all the time, even if it's negative, you're self-centered. Today, notice how often you think or stress about yourself. What is one way you could reframe those thoughts today?

_____
_____
_____
_____
_____
_____
_____
_____
_____

"Self care requires neither explanation nor justification."
- **Unknown**

Affirmation

Today, I embrace the care I deserve, cherishing moments of joy and self-nurturing activities. I express gratitude for my body, treating it like a precious temple, prioritizing healthy nourishment, ample rest, and physical well-being. I limit exposure to negativity and practice mindfulness and meditation, I'm grateful for the peace and clarity they bring.

Action Prompt

Self-care is not selfish, it's essential. We all need care for our emotional health and physical health. It's also critical to take time for introspection. When you think about your self-care routine, does it need improvement? What is one way you can practice self-care today?

_____
_____
_____
_____
_____
_____
_____
_____
_____
_____
_____
_____
_____

"Sometimes gratitude won't find you but you can find gratitude."
- **Unknown**

Affirmation

Today, I cultivate an attitude of gratitude by keeping a gratitude journal and practicing mindfulness. I will express gratitude to those I care about and writing thank you notes whenever necessary. I will make an effort to return to gratitude even if I stray for a little while. I know that while I won't feel grateful every minute, a few small actions can help me find it again.

Action Prompt

The quote suggests that gratitude is not always automatic and that we must actively seek it out, especially when things are challenging. It notes the power of a positive perspective and the impact it has on our wellbeing. What do you do when you don't feel grateful? What is one action you can take right now to return yourself to gratitude?

"You are the average of the 5 people closest to you."
– Jim Rohn

Affirmation

Today, I recognize the profound influence of the five people closest to me. These individuals are not only a reflection of my character but also play a vital role in shaping my path of growth and self-improvement. I am grateful for the positive impact they bring into my life, for they inspire me to be better, foster gratitude, and encourage my continuous evolution.

Action Prompt

The people you spend the most time with have a significant impact on your thoughts, beliefs, and habits. You will become like the people you surround yourself with, so choose them wisely. Take a moment to assess the people in your world. Do they lift you up or drag you down? If you think they drag you down, what is one way you can avoid them today?

_____

_____

_____

_____

_____

_____

_____

_____

_____

_____

"If you don't make time for your wellness you will be forced to make time for your illness."
- Unknown

Affirmation

Today, I commit to my wellness. I will take care of my mental health and physical health. I will show gratitude to myself by making sure I get the care I need. I will remember to take breaks, to breathe, and to ask for help when I need it. I know I don't have to do any of this alone and will reach out to others for support when I struggle.

Action Prompt

As James Clear says, "Every action you take is a vote for the person you want to become." Make good votes for yourself. What are your health and wellness goals? Are you working towards them? What is one small action you can take towards a wellness goal. Examples: breathe deeply a few times more today, one push up, anything that gets you started.

_____
_____
_____
_____
_____
_____
_____
_____

"You can have everything you want in life if you will just help other people get what they want."

– Zig Ziglar

Affirmation

Today, I will help others achieve what they want knowing that helping others will only strengthen my path. I know what I want is coming and my hard work will pay off and I will not let that distract me from supporting my loved ones and colleagues. I know I can help the people I care about reach their goals and I will make that a priority in my life.

Action Prompt

Being selfish and self-absorbed will hurt your journey more than it will help it. Helping others will not only help you get what you want but will help make you feel more satisfied along the way. How can you help people in your life? What is something you can do today to support someone else in their vision?

_____
_____
_____
_____
_____
_____
_____
_____
_____

"Life is what your thoughts make it."
- Marcus Aurelius

Affirmation

Today, I will make my thoughts positive and help my brain live in peace and serenity. I will focus on gratitude and helping others knowing that will return to me. Even when my thoughts stray into the darkness, I will not panic. I will reset and bring my mind back into a healthy place, as many times as I need to throughout the day.

Action Prompt

Was it a bad day or are you just milking it all day? We get to choose how we feel about everything in life. No one else. What are your thoughts like throughout the day? Are they mostly positive or negative? What is a positive thought you could have for today? Practice coming back to it even when your mind wanders.

"Sometimes what you're looking for is already there."
- Arthur Franklin

Affirmation

Today, I will be grateful for what I have and consider that what I'm looking for is in my life. I will re-evaluate my priorities and goals, and see if what I'm searching for is already present. I will take a moment to practice gratitude and appreciation for what I already have. If I feel myself moving away from gratitude, I will pause and reset.

Action Prompt

The grass is greener where you water it. Stop imagining that it's greener somewhere else. If you find yourself constantly searching for people, places and things to feel fulfilled, you might want to consider that the problem is in you. Take a moment and think about what you have and what you want. Where's the overlap? What is one thing you can do today to practice appreciation for what you already have?

"You cannot be lonely if you like the person you are alone with."
- Wayne Dyer

Affirmation

Today, I remind myself that who I am is enough. I will practice enjoying my time alone and doing activities i enjoy. If moments arise where I feel lonely or stressed, I will remind myself that they will pass and I'm working on self-appreciation and self-care. I will honor who I am by feeling confident about myself and what I bring to this world.

Action Prompt

If you are at peace with yourself and have a positive relationship with your own thoughts and emotions, being alone can be an enjoyable and fulfilling experience. You are what you think about, so think good thoughts about yourself. Take a moment and reflect on a couple of your best qualities. What is something you can do today to show gratitude for yourself?

_____
_____
_____
_____
_____
_____
_____
_____
_____
_____

"What separates privilege from entitlement is gratitude."
- Brene Brown

Affirmation
Today, I will practice gratitude for my life. I will acknowledge and be thankful for what the universe has given me. I choose to see everything that is blessed about my life today. If I get into moments of irritability, or start to feel entitled, I will pause and remember to be grateful for my life and my blessings.

Action Prompt
In our culture of more, more, more, it's easy to forget to be grateful and proud of what you have. If you have enough to eat, wear, and people who love you that is privilege. Make no mistake about that. What are the blessings in your life? How can you let the people who love you know that you are grateful for them today?

_____
_____
_____
_____
_____
_____
_____
_____
_____
_____
_____
_____

> **"If another person is responsible for the fulfillment of your joy you're never going to be fully satisfied."**
> – Wayne Dyer

Affirmation

I have the power to be in control of my own feelings. I know that no one else can make me whole or happy. I have the strength to be OK today no matter what happens with other people. Other people do not have the power to steal my joy. I am the master of my mind and my emotions.

Action Prompt

This is a trap many fall into—letting another person, or persons, be responsible for your happiness. Be the master of your own happiness. Don't wait for others to bring joy into your life. Remember, true satisfaction comes from within. Do you notice that you let others affect your happiness? What is something you can do today to take control and be accountable for your own emotions?

_____
_____
_____
_____
_____
_____
_____
_____
_____

> "Be yourself; everyone else is already taken."
> – Oscar Wilde

Affirmation

Today, I honor who I am. I will be true to myself rather than trying to imitate or conform to others. I will feel proud of my uniqueness. I know that no one else has to offer what I do. I will recognize that I am special and I will choose to see that what makes me different makes me wonderful. I will be grateful about everything I am and have to bring to the world.

Action Prompt

There is only one version of you and that is your gift. You have no competition and you should embrace and be proud of your unique qualities, characteristics, and personalities. Being original is more fulfilling than trying to be someone else. What makes you unique? Is there some small way you can honor that today?

_____
_____
_____
_____
_____
_____
_____
_____
_____
_____
_____

> "The unhappiest people in this world, are those who care the most about what other people think."
> - C. Joybell

Affirmation

Today, I will not obsess over what other people think. I know other people's opinions of me are none of my business. What someone else thinks does not change anything, good or bad. I feel strong in my own thinking and decision making. I trust myself to do the right thing and I will focus only on myself and what I need to do.

Action Prompt

Individuals who constantly seek validation and approval from others tend to be the least content with their lives. It's critical to not let other's opinions dictate one's own happiness. Focusing too much on other's thoughts can lead to unhappiness. How can you stay in your own lane? What is one thing to do today to stay focused on yourself?

> **"You are the most influential person you will talk to all day. Listen to yourself."**
> - Unknown

Affirmation

I recognize that I am the most influential person I will engage with throughout the day. I choose to speak to myself with kindness, encouragement, and gratitude. By fostering a positive inner dialogue, I cultivate resilience, confidence, and a joyful mindset. Today, I embrace the profound impact of my self-talk and use it to shape my thoughts and actions in a way that aligns with my goals and well-being.

Action Prompt

Reflect on the conversations you have with yourself throughout the day. Are your thoughts primarily positive or negative? Think about the most influential person you will talk to all day – you. What is one small action you can take today to make your self-talk more supportive, kind, and grateful?

_____
_____
_____
_____
_____
_____
_____
_____

"Growth always hurts."
- Unknown

Affirmation

Today, I know that progress comes with challenges and discomfort. With each moment of growth, I am thankful for the strength and resilience it cultivates within me. I choose to see the pain as a sign of progress, a reminder that I am continually evolving and expanding. Gratitude is my guiding light on this journey of growth, and I welcome it with an open heart.

Action Prompt

Reflect on a recent challenge you faced and the valuable lessons it brought, along with any moments of gratitude you experienced during or after overcoming it. Now, consider a current challenge in your life. How can you use your past lessons, along with a mindset of gratitude, to tackle this new hurdle?

"A truly happy person is one who can enjoy the scenery on a detour."
- Unknown

Affirmation

Today, I understand that happiness isn't solely found in reaching a destination but in appreciating the beauty of the journey, even when it takes unexpected turns. I welcome detours as an opportunity for growth. I choose to find joy in the unexpected and savor the unique scenery these detours offer and I cultivate a spirit of gratitude that enriches my life.

Action Prompt

Consider a recent life detour. How did you handle it, and what did you learn? How can you find joy in unexpected twists today?

"No one ever went broke or got poor helping others."
- Unknown

Affirmation

Today, I choose to be a source of aid and kindness, knowing that my actions contribute to a world of plenty. As I give, I receive in gratitude and blessings, ensuring that no one ever goes poor or broke when they help others. By extending my hand to support and uplift those in need, I make a positive impact and open the door to a life rich in gratitude and prosperity.

Action Prompt

Recall how helping others has enriched your life in the past, whether through a small gesture or a significant effort. Find a meaningful way to assist someone today, embracing the profound sense of gratitude that accompanies such acts of kindness.

_____
_____
_____
_____
_____
_____
_____
_____
_____
_____
_____

ACKNOWLEDGEMENTS

I extend heartfelt gratitude to my family, friends, and coworkers who have accompanied me on this transformative journey, shaping the person I am today.

A special tribute to the remarkable community of over 100 Navy SEALs I've had the privilege to work with, entrusting me with their stories and placing their trust in me through my role on the Board of the SEAL Future Foundation. I am honored to contribute by offering guidance and mentorship to these elite individuals.

Metallica, whose music has shaped the chapters of my life, I am deeply grateful for the opportunity to contribute to your world through my role on the Advisory Board of the All Within My Hands Foundation.

I want to express my deepest thanks to Lindsey & Leslie Glass from Reach Out Recovery for their brilliance and expertise, which played a pivotal role in bringing this book to its final form.

For more information, visit: www.thesoberexec.com

ABOUT THE AUTHOR

Chris Anthony is a dedicated leader, speaker, author, podcaster, mentor, and lifelong learner with a passion for serving others. Boasting 25 years of business experience, he is an accomplished tech executive and was employee #192 at ExactTarget, a company later acquired by Salesforce in 2013 for $2.5 billion.

In addition to his professional accomplishments, Chris is actively engaged in various non-profit organizations. He proudly serves on the advisory boards of Metallica's All Within My Hands Foundation and the Los Angeles Sports and Entertainment Commission (LASEC). Furthermore, he holds the role of Board Member at the SEAL Future Foundation (SFF), actively supporting U.S. Navy SEALs in transitioning to successful business careers. In this capacity, Chris plays a vital role in actively supporting elite professionals in their transition to successful business careers.

Currently residing in Los Angeles with his wife and two children, Chris continues to embody the principles of leadership, mentorship, and service in both his personal and professional life.

www.ingramcontent.com/pod-product-compliance
Lightning Source LLC
Chambersburg PA
CBHW072211070526
44585CB00015B/1287